11

BOOK II

HOME

Let me live here I don't want to be alone
My heart is in your hands and that is my home
every moment I've spent with you
made all my dreams come true

Let me stay here right by your side
I have no secrets that linger or hide
I'm happy right where I am
my hearts my home and it's in your hands

I am at home
I am at home
When I'm with you

Everywhere you go you'd never leave me alone
because you know that you are my home
you are always where I want to be
together forever just you and me...

S.H.

SUPERNATURAL

Ft. CORDELL of Eliteskill.com

You're so annoying
boy you be lying
give you props for trying
never denying
yet something attracts me
gets me
flaunting
hopelessly

I want you but I don't
want to touch you, but I won't
swallow my pride
choking down my throat

(CORDELL)

I, I, I
want you all
but I'm afraid I may fall
you always pick up when I call
but it may be a scene from saw
maybe not at all

I don't want to be played again
I believe that you would make this a sin
a regret that I will forever hold within
while I cry your ass will have the biggest grin

S.H.

UNFAITHFUL

The time has come for us to say goodbye (goodbye)
the time has come for us to say goodnight (goodnight)
I'm leaving you behind with the memories
I'm leaving you behind so you can see
what you've done to me
unfaithful
unfaithful
unfaithfulness

There's something I can't get out my mind
you fucked up really bad this time
didn't care if there's things I would find
but it was only a matter of time
unfaithful
unfaithful
unfaithful bliss

S.H.

TAKE THAT BACK TRACK

take that back track
take that back track
take that back track

Now that it's done and over
now a new life commence
let me try this while I'm sober
the beginning of romance
every time I move forward
you make me take two steps back
when I thought it was over
I take that back track

take that back track
take that back track
take that back track

Creeping undercover
hiding what I left behind
thought it was over
apparently I'm not that hard to find

Got me looking over my shoulders
got you creeping in my head
with the strength of a boulder
I want you to squash me dead

take that back track
take that back track

S.H.

BEFORE I HAVE TO GO

Remember the things that I would fear
these little things you should know
maybe I wasn't very clear
remember me before I have to go

I'll take everything that I'm allowed
to where ever I may rest
peaceful slumber this I know
maybe this is the best

I know I am already late
I have passed with little excuses
Know this life was great
I learned how to abuse it

Sweet sorrow for who I left behind
sweet sorry for those who don't know
It was finally my time
to go

We will meet I know at the end
I will greet you for there's things I'll show
my unsettled family, friend
before you have to go...

S.H.

CRAZY BUTTERCUP

You call me crazy
I wrote a poem about it
but your ass is lazy
you barely get excited
I don't know why
but I love it
I think we both are crazy
I like when we be fightin'

Love when you yell than stutter
forget what you were about to say
stubble upon your words even better
I guess we both cray, cray
but love we love each other

Crazy, crazy, crazy
than you call me buttercup
one moment your angry
and than you're up my butt
I love these moments
and than I laugh
making you so mad
you want to kick my ass
crazy, crazy, buttercup

S.H.

FADING (HURRY UP)

You told me you love me and you would never let me go
What of all that shit you said was it all for show
I'm not playing
my minds made up
I'm just saying
don't give up
if this love is fading
than it hurry up

I got no time for loser, abusers in my life
I've been done that in the past and last night
that's right

You told me you love me and you would never let me go
What of all that shit you said was it all for show

S.H.

NO TIME FOR US

Did my best for this love
he put me through the test for this love
I did my best for this love
but I wasn't meant to be loved

He did his thing
he went his way
I was left behind
with nothing to say

*You went here
you went there
leaving no time for us to share
did you care
that this wasn't fair
that our love went everywhere*

I stayed at home
at times I felt alone
though you where here
felt like you disappeared

To find you moved on
and kept me to the side
now I'm struggling
while you're happy
at someone else side...

S.H.

*Taken form the Poem: I'VE BEEN SPENDING A LONG TIME
From the poetry book: 1976

SPACE (CONDENSED)

I want to creep in your mind
Wish I could do it sometimes
and hear the words that speak before you do
so I can counter attack you

Space
is all we need
space
from you and me
space
in between
I'm not trying to be mean

We just need time
from what's really on our mind
one day I hope you'll find
that I was always yours
and you were always mine...

S.H.

WORSE LOVE

A year has passed
and you're still in my mind
how much longer will it last
how much more in time

I can't move on, coming back to you
deep inside I think you feel it too
I wannabe with you
worse love

Fix what you broke
you left me crying
was it a joke

Repair my broken heart
tape it if you will
staple, glue anything
even kill

Don't leave it for someone else
it was your job
trash talking
worse love

S.H.

FOR I LOVED

For I loved him
more than anyone could ever loved
I gave him everything
except the stars above
I never denied him
when I should have
but I know him
and for this I'm glad
Learned my lesson
learned it very well
as I continue making mistakes
there's no one I could tell
did this on my own
I do not know why
I have yet to be grown
I have yet to open my eyes
I know my failures
and I know my strengths
which was made for me tailored
I will never learn
I will always fail
life for me was a lesson alone
this you can tell

S.H.

LUNASCAPE

I lay here and close my eyes
concentrate on all my tries
playing back my life
where I have failed
to many mistakes
to follow one trail
to many faults
to ever derail

I never ended
where I began
I don't know where
I lost my confidence

They have said you will learn
from your mistakes
if I have
I wouldn't be in this place
maybe I am attracted
to what I fear
which is basically failing
my family, friends and anyone near

I never began
where I ended
I know no one cares
if I ever mended

S.H.

YOUR OWN SHADOW

I didn't eat
so I went walking
baring my feet
on the pavement talking
no one else around
but felt someone stalking
dark figure creep
very haunting

I didn't sleep
had to much on my mind
went to the kitchen
turning on the lights
there it stood
there it's watches
nothing could be good
as it approaches

I could not hide
I could not run
no matter where I went
no matter how I could confront

This pattern was messing with my head
stalking me like a sparrow
when life makes you fear
your own shadow…

S.H.

□□ALWAYS□□□□□□□□

I burned myself like a photograph
hoping the memories will not last
I tried to scratch off every picture with your face
but there were reminders in every place

tearing up everything that reminds
me of those once good times
than all of a sudden it came to me
that I was the one bringing forth these haunting memories

September
October
when you said goodbye
forever
together
I will swallow my pride

Found what I thought I was looking for
someone unlike you, with something more
but your memories they just flushed in
filled my memories, feels like I'm drowning

It was October when you said you wanted to leave
not September as I always believed
imagining you until my head bleeds
what have you done, what have you done to me?

S.H.

TWINKLE

I see the twinkle in your eyes
every time
you're at my side
I see the smile
that fills my day
it's been awhile
as far as I could say

Erasing the past
where I did wrong
where I was done wrong
hope this feeling lasts
and keeps going strong

I see the twinkle in your eyes
which gets me by
this hell we call life
and strife
everything is alright
when you're at my side
and when I see
the twinkle in your eyes...

S.H.

WHAT YOU MEAN TO ME

This feels right
you're so far out of sight
so far from what I could ever dream
and in between

I've never felt like this before
a lover, friend, my world and more
creating new memories
outstanding dreams

You've opened my eyes to a whole new world
a new experience and change I've never felt before
and when you call out my name
I don't feel a shame

loving and so kind
with an outstanding mind
I love you and you love me
all the time

When we touch
there is too much
yet theirs just us

This is where I want to be
loving you, you loving me
forever it may seem
you're just a dream
dream to me...

S.H.

ITS YOU (FOR ME)

It's true
that I'm in love with you
and everything that you do
for me

So you
take my by the hand
happy to be your man
it's where I want to be

Everything seems in place
loving your heavenly embrace
when you touch upon my face
like you do

It's you
all you
and the things you do
for me

S.H.

THROUGH THE HOURGLASS

It's like sands through an hourglass
when you learn everything never lasts
when lessons teach you in time
and makes you realize
that you are fine
better left alone
with lesson yet to unfold
with thorns from a rose
or when life has it's holes

Keep on moving
it'll be tricky
like a roller-coaster ride
that has it's up and downs
be happy, be happy that you're still around

For you will learn
for you will yearn
to strive upon the great
making stupid mistakes
but don't falter
don't let it bother
your ride

Nothing will be safe
yet you will strive
like sands through the hourglass
and so are the days of our lives…

S.H.

□□□□□□□

Hurry up
I'm falling in love with you
Giving up
Is what I'm trying not to do
Stirring up
this thing between me and you
Standing here
looking like a fool
falling with you like it's summertime
longing you
like it is a winter crime
waiting to see what you do
I'll wait forever if I have the time

Love the little things you say
when you smile and look my way
I think about you
every night and day
what more can I say
I'm in love
I'm in need
I'm right here
can't you see
me..
me..
me.

S.H.

LETHAL

I gave all that I could give
I lived your life the way I could live
followed your every footsteps
snow, sand, pavement
even tho I hated it

I crumpled and you did not care
I began hiding emotions I didn't want to share
even though you were there

Gave all I could
stand by your side as I should
take a bullet for you, I would
but I was never any good

I changed just to be you
I rearranged my life to fit your style
and all this I went through
all you could do is smile

I regret nothing
I hold on to nothing
there will be no sequel
because what you have done
was very lethal...

S.H.

WHAT YOU'VE DONE

What you've done to me was totally wrong
and now I'm writing it in this poem
the dream I had was so unclear
I thought you would be forever with me, here
I guess it came clear to you

the pain still lingers deep inside
because I don't know the reason why
that you've done what you did
to me

I'll be fine
hoping in time
reliving in rhymes
but you wanted you more
than what I could ever have in store
so you went your way
and left me in the rain
there's nothing I wanted more
than you...

S.H.

DO YOU HEAR MY HEART

Do you hear my heart beating
can you feel it deep inside
there's no way we could keep screaming
and expect one of us to be alive

This torment you call relationship
this hatred deep in your soul
I always knew you hate it
maybe that was your planned goal

I began to count backwards
I began to lose my steps
contemplating your standards
left with a bag of regrets

I won't wait for you
I won't stand on you
I will move on through
ignore the things you do

do you feel my heart beating
do you understand why
I don't this feeling
all I could do is cry...

S. H.

NEVER GOOD ENOUGH

What my friend told me were all true
no matter what I do fits you
the fighting, arguing is making me weak
to the point I can't get through and speak
no matter what I have done
there is always a game for you to be won

cook, clean
wait at your feet
vacuum, broom, dishes
I'm not your genie to grant you wishes

It's all true
you did you
you're fake

I need you
I'm here for you
are words you can't say

Like the seasons change
yet you remain
I'm always the blame
such a shame

S.H.

LOVELY THING

There is something in your eyes
that makes me feel that everything will be alright

there's something in your soul
that won't let me go

emotionally attached as we can be
just you and me

free

S.H.

FORTY-THREE (43)

I'm forty-three and lonely
I had all the love yet only
one tore it apart

forty-three years of me
forty-three more
hopefully

now I stand in grand
with the one in hand
my man

nothing could stand in my way
I know this is love and that's all I have to say
I don't have to prove myself
or be another doll on someones shelf

forty-three
finding love
was always
me...

S.H.

SPECIAL TO ME

Thanks for taking me in
and giving me a chance
the love you have for me
and our special romance
I will never forget
I shall never regret
what you have done
my hearts the reward you have won

hopefully one day you'll see
how special
how special you are to me...

S.H.

YOU ARE

You made me this way
you started
now your words are gray
and discarded

Are you even here
have you even noticed
that I will soon disappear
leaving you novice

A breath away from saying goodbye
my ride awaits, outside
don't hold me back I'm about to go
you don't even know

Loser is what my friends would say
if I stay
so since you don't care
guess I'll be outta here…

S.H.

SINCE THE DAY

you took my hand
and decided I would be your man
and lifted me from the hell I became
you showered your love
like if it was rain
brought the sun into my life
calmed my storms and my strife
eased my pain and made me smile
since the day we met
you loved me
and not for awhile
feels like eternity when you're around
taming the winds with your soft spoken sound
make me look forward to another day
I love you more than any poem could say...

S.H.

I lived what I learned
never stolen but earned
the passions of life
that I dearly hold inside
mistakes have been made
the sun played it's shade
but I am still here
or I will always be near...

S.H.

passion with hate
strife and life
nothing compares
to the day but what holds the night
forever lingering in my hands
are the hearts of so many yet slipping like sand
this was never met for me
it was never met to be
but at least I know
that one day I will be free

S.H.

MY BEDROOM

Sitting here in my bedroom contemplating
thinking back, of when we were in love
I knew I fucked up when I was compensating
now I'm dwelling in the reminiscence of
I stopped breathing
I stopped screaming
I stopped cheating
I stopped bleeding

In my bedroom, here all alone
remembering when you were my own
like a king without his thrown
I miss you being home

My own prison
is where I be
in the bedroom
once you, now just me...

S.H.

SANTOS HERNANDEZ

www.ingramcontent.com/pod-product-compliance
Lightning Source LLC
Chambersburg PA
CBHW031618040426
42452CB00006B/577